# TRICK and TRAPPED into POVERTY

## DARRON DESHUNN

# TRICK AND TRAPPED INTO POVERTY

## DARRON DESHUNN

Copyright @2020 by Darron Deshunn

All rights reserved. No part of this book may be reproduced in any form or by any electronic or mechanical means, including information storage and retrieval systems, without permission in writing from the publisher, except by reviewers, who may quote brief passages in a review.

This publication contains the opinions and ideas of its author. It is intended to provide helpful and informative material on the subjects addressed in the publication. The author and publisher specifically disclaim all responsibility for any liability, loss or risk, personal or otherwise, which is incurred as a consequence, directly or indirectly, of the use and application of any of the contents of this book.

WORKBOOK PRESS LLC
187 E Warm Springs Rd,
Suite B285, Las Vegas, NV 89119, USA

Website:   https://workbookpress.com/
Hotline:   1-888-818-4856
Email:     admin@workbookpress.com

Ordering Information:
Quantity sales. Special discounts are available on quantity purchases by corporations, associations, and others. For details, contact the publisher at the address above.

ISBN-13:   978-1-953839-85-5 (Paperback Version)
           978-1-953839-86-2 (Digital Version)
           978-1-954753-58-7 (Hardback Version)

REV. DATE: 26.09.2020

# CONTENTS

**Dedicated** •••••••••••••••••••• **04**

**Introduction** •••••••••••••••••• **05**

## CHAPTER 1

Cracked skull ••••••••••••••••• 07

Drinking A Cup Of Bleach ••••••• 07

Cut finger ••••••••••••••••••• 07

Marble in the nostril •••••••••• 07

Holding a chair •••••••••••••••• 08

Darkest moment •••••••••••••••• 08

I remember lots happy moments •• 08

My First bike ••••••••••••••••• 08

Late 1976 moved to Compton ca. ••• 08

Bus riding A •••••••••••••••••• 09

"sympatric" moment •••••••••••• 09

Compton court disruption •••••••• 10

Bully ••••••••••••••••••••••• 10

I love music ••••••••••••••••• 10

## CHAPTER 2

Moved to watts. ••••••••••••••• 11

Grandma Passed away •••••••••• 11

Great cook ••••••••••••••••••• 12

"Nicknames" •••••••••••••••••• 12

New school,# 5 ••••••••••••••• 12

Baseball .................................................. 13

## CHAPTER 3

"Rake the yard" ........................................ 15

Fun places ............................................... 15

Water head .............................................. 16

Junior high school. 6 ................................. 16

Poverty realized, ...................................... 16

## CHAPTER 4

School number 7 ...................................... 19

1984 summertime "you must be crazy" ....... 19

PRO basketball ........................................ 20

"You better know what you are doing" ....... 20

1984 Here's Some of the Famous Cruel Ridiculous Remarks. ... 21

"You Aint Going To Be Shit" ..................... 21

The Component set, TV and VCR. ............ 21

Bicycling Lucky me .................................. 21

I still got some sanity laft. ......................... 21

## CHAPTER 5

High School, number 9. ............................ 22

1987 On the move again, new school number 9 ... 22

1987 Officially a high school drop out ...... 23

Eighteen years old .................................... 23

## CHAPTER 6

Back from san Bernardino ............ 26
1990 "There Were A Couple Of Memorable Outing" .... 26
Family outing, to the batting cage ........ 26
Major league baseball game. ........... 27
1990 Meet My Second Real Girl Friend ...... 27

## CHAPTER 7

I'm retired ..................... 30
Tough job ..................... 30
I've worked in some nice places, super markets, banks, studios, .. 30
County jail vacation ................ 31
"Penthouse living at its finest". .......... 32

## CHAPTER 8

Came down sick .................. 34
Passed way .................... 35
I sold my classical car. .............. 35

## CHAPTER 9

"Now I know" ................... 36
The Epitaph .................... 38
Book quiz ..................... 40

# DEDICATED

I wont to dedicate my autobiography to all my well – wishers as while as those who prayed and supported me though many trials and tribulations. And last but not least "the great city of Los Angeles", California. MY Home howntown.

**"THANK YOU SO MUCH"**

# INTRODUCTION

What if some one walked up to you while you are working and said "are you a where that you are a BENJAMIN FRANKLIN descendent". the number one American and founding father of the united states of America. the great inventor, scientist, writer. ECT.

Your reaction would probably be along this line, Wow! Where do I go to cash in or, where do I go to reap the benefits. Hold on you are the from the dark side of the united states of American. You represent salvery. 50 /50 maulatto the gray in between the black and white, a breed.

Hello, my DARRON DESHUNN, This is my Autobiography, Deposition. I was born on February 18th 1970, In los angels, Cailfornia, where have resided my whole life. I grew up in poverty in the city's of Compton, south Los Angeles, Watts. I'm the youngest of seven siblings. A high school drops out in 10th grade. However I went back to school to get my GED in 2005.

My parent were both from little rock, Arkansas. they also raised In poverty, they both **picked cotton** in the field, while they kids. my mother could read but was not highly educated, My father was **uneducated.**

My mother was an affectionate house wife. My father was a machinist, junkman, before I was born my family moved to Los Angeles California 1969.

I would describe my self as. Handsome and attractive with a strong resemblance to Benjamin Franklin, my face and body are very distinctive. very Appeasing, easy to befriend. Fun – Loving, I like to smile and laugh., Respectful. I treat everyone the same. Hi, Hello, How are you doing? ECT

## "Hi Darron Deshunn Mucho Gusto."

I know slavery is still a very sensitive subject. and will cause controversy. there is much resentment on both sides and people will still argue the facts.

**I Do Not Intend To Cause Any Grief, Hate OR Harm Onto Any One.**

My goal is to detach for myself from our founding fathers sex scandals. And leave **"positive legacy".**

# CHAPTER 1

My most memorable memories, those are the memories that molded me into the person that I' am today, I remember them like yesterday. Some are riddled with pain, some are riddled with joy, a few seem humiliate, others seem to annoy. The One that stuck out the most happened in nineteen seven p h o.

When I was between age 4 and 6. I loved to explorer and required lots of attention. I was dangerous and injurious to myself and sometimes others. Ending up in the emergency room four times. Here are the injuries. Starting With the most painful one first.

## CRACKED SKULL

1974 When I was 4yeares old, I remember throwing rocks in our front yard with my brother, (rip), the next thing I remember is being hit square in forehead. with huge rock which cracked my skull and sent to the emergency room where it took several stitches to close the wound. The mark is still on my forehead.

## DRINKING A CUP OF BLEACH

1975 I remember walking into kitchen picking up cup of up off the table and tacking a swallow if bleach, all I remember is vomiting out of control.

## CUT FINGER

Cut finger 1976 I loved trying thing that were dangerous, I remember filling one of those old 5 gallon water bottles and than trying to move it. I may have been strong but not that strong I tried to lift it. I was able to clear the ground, however it dropped out of hands busted and cut middle finger causing another trip to emergency room for several stitches.

## MARBLE IN THE NOSTRIL

Marble in the nostril 1976 One day while playing in the house alone I wondered upon my brother's bag of marbles. I picked them up and opened the bag "oh what are those"? What are they for? Lets try this sticking one up my nostril uh oh I cant get it out. Mommy as ran scared to pointing to my nose, she had no luck getting it out, Wouldn't you know it another trip to the emergency room.

## HOLDING A CHAIR

Holding a chair 1976 I remember being suspended from school, for holding chair over a student head. When the teacher stepped of the class.

## DARKEST MOMENTS

1976 My most darkest moments it was the one and only time mom tried to wipe me in 1976 she held the belt in one hand and me by the arm with the other. she started swing, I reached back with closed fist striking her in jaw the she stopped. went got from the other room he came in and my dad and finished. one of the worse wiping I ever got. Something we never talked about again.

## I REMEMBER LOTS HAPPY MOMENTS MY FIRST BIKE

1975 like when my father brought me my first bicycle when I was 5 years old, I remember riding it up and down and the street. Every since than I've love to ride. It one of my favorite hobbies to this day.

1975 I remember sleeping in between them because the house was crowed. with all of my siblings were still at home. That, I think spoiled me.

1975 I remember starting school (kindergarten). my best year of school I will never forget thanksgiving when my teacher made a pumpkin pie and shared it with the whole class. It was delicious.

## LATE **1976** MOVE TO COMPTON

1976 I remember moving to Compton, Ca. thus; I had to changed schools. My third in two years. It ends up being my favorite of the places of all the places we lived. My brother and I made good friends, we were close all together there were six of us, I was youngest.

1977 we lived right across from the railroad tracks. In front in apartment apt. 1, we stayed in Compton about years. And enjoyed every moment of it. The summer time was the best time, because we were out school.

## BUS RIDING

1977 we would ride the bus all over from long beach to los angels, none stop. Either we would find the transfers or ask the bus driver to for free ride, we rode everyday, most of the bus drive knew us, and would say no, we would just wait for next bus or catch one going in different direction. we stayed on the move.

1977 Compton was the place I first begin playing sports, I will away remember going the Compton high school, to play throw up tackle football, I loved it, I remember scoring my first touchdown it was also my first catch. the ball was hiked I was the outside I took off running looked back the ball the ball was in the air I put hands up grabbed it and kept running, touchdown! My first score.

1977 At school I used play on the monkey bars. Learned all the flips I'm not trying to brag but I was as good as anybody in the school on the monkey's bars.

## A "SYMPATRIC" MOMENT

1978 I remember going to a parade with my mom and brother (rip) on Compton blvd in front on the library next to the court house. I remember there we are standing in front row of people. I look up what do see two lady connected by the top of there heads riding slowly in the back of convertible car.

1978 There were Siamese twins and African American. I froze and just stared at them for a moment, I could not believe what I was seeing, I guess that feeling was called "sympathy". After all those lady bonded together for life, obviously they couldn't do anything that we are accustomed to doing. I wish there was something I could have done comfort them.

1978 a few second after, a parade clown walked up to me and said "you know what you look just like me" that embarrassed me which was easy to do because I was very shay kid.

## COMPTON COURT DISRUPTION

1978 If our crew had one fault, we were bit to this disruptive. Example after school if we were bored, We would walk down the street, to the Compton court house, I think we figured since it's the tallest building in the city, why not go there sometime to play.

1978 we would go there and run up and the stairs. Go up and down elevators, yelling and horse playing all down hallways. Since we were running through hallways the deputies could not catch us, but they could hear all the noise as we passed.

1978 We run in and the out doors, we did it several times before they were able catch us, they could not catch us in building they caught us leaving the property. The first time the deputy was very polite, A week later we went back.

1978 We thought they would forget. they didn't, we were caught again this time the the deputy threaten two take the two oldest to juvenile hall. My brother was one two oldest. So that was our last time we there as one unit.

## BULLY

1978 I had reputation as a bully, my friend would put me up to fight for no reason. I remember one day, we were walking by from playing football at Compton high school. There was kid playing alone in his yard. He was shorter but heavier than was.

1978 One of friends said "Darron go get him "with out thinking, I walked into his yard and started fighting with him. That kid was nobody to play with. He beat me soundly. And I learned valuable lesson that has lasted me for life, Respect others and never underestimate anybody. Just because he didn't look tough then not he wasn't tough.

## I LOVE MUSIC

1979 where started listening to music, I remember my brother and I and would stay home alone. listening to music every since I've been a very big fan of all type music. I have many good memories from Compton.

# CHAPTER 2

## MOVED TO WATTS

1979 Time to move, once again which means a new school, number 4 this is the hardest on me its middle of the school year, this school has many more kids, aim shay so don't make friends easily.

1980 So I felt lost. and wouldn't not get any better the rest of year.

1980 I missed tmy old neighborhood, I was use to I coming home throwing my stuff down and going right back outside to meet my friends. I did not have friends yet and brother was still in school. I didn't believe in home work so what can I do. Nothing but hang with mom which was cool. She had me spoiled at the time, If she had it then I could get it.

## GRANDMA PASSED AWAY

1980 My Grandma on my mother side passed away of cancer at age seven two. I remember my mother crying that was the first and last time I ever seen my mother cry. She got a call from my uncle who was at the hospital when my Grandmother dead. We all were up stairs. I remember my mom hanging up the phone, than she walked into the rest room for few moments. then came out shedding tears, I remember my brother walked up to her hugged her and said "mom it ok". She replied in a low sad voice "poor mother".

1980 I grand mother was at this time in the late seventies, she was like beg lady. When she visited she brought her youngest son which was my uncle of course. He had a mental problem. He would rock back and forward on the couch. I asked my mother what wrong with him?, my mom replied "She (Grandmother) would not take him to the doctor. When he was little boy. He was sick with a had very high fever. It did something to his mind". Was a mulatto.

1980 the thing I most remember about my grand mother was the sneak that she would bring me, it was always stale, but didn't mind I just wonted the prize in the box, I will never forget her nickname for me "Bonnie Google". I will never forget my Grand mother.

# GREAT COOK

1980 my mom was a "great cook", everything she cooked was very good, starting with my favorite, pinto beans and buttermilk cornbread out of cast a iron skillet and baked or fried chicken. Or her home made meat loaf with mashed potatoes. she mostly cooked soul food but every once an a while she would cook spaghetti.

1980 She wa also very good at preparing thanksgiving and charismas dinners, I don't think any body could beat her tradition turkey dressing with gravy. Potato salad it was outstanding.

1980 breakfast was special as while, my favorite was her smothered potatoes with again home made buttermilk biscuits with salmon croquettes, yummy. What about her pancakes with beacon and scrambled eggs.

1980 Her Pastries were unrivaled starting with her sweet potato pies, and peach and black berries cobblers. bananas pudding. Yummy. To me my mom was best cook in the world. Thanks mom.

# "NICKNAMES"

My mom didn't nickname the kids negatively, but she did have nicknames for my two of cousins, my cousin girl she nicknamed Sally, My boy cousin she nicknamed Peter

# NEW SCHOOL, #5

1981 what did school mean?, running, laughing, and food, briefest pancakes, lunch hamburgers. that all I knew. My new school I got conferrable quickly, At the beginning of year all the kids are new.

So I fitted right in, found some kids who have the same interest as I did. football and that year I started playing basketball. fun, fun.

1981 My fifth teacher she was from the old school meaning she believed in corporal punishment. She was also was a **outstanding teacher**, I learn few things in class room, like long division, along with the normal curriculum,

I remember her telling me after checking my work "Darron" you are not afraid of big numbers in a complimentary way. That made me feel smart.

1981 She was also no none since. I remember after pulling to side,. so not to embrace me, she said "Darron you are a nice looking, but don't smile so much I makes you look ugly". I think she got tired hear me laugh so much.

1981 I also I remember her wooden peddle her, that swing like power hitting baseball player. I can't count the times I got spanker, No question I would allow any of kids to attend her class as 5 grader. Thanks

1982 I liked to draw football men when class was doing school work, I would draw and think about what mom was cooking for dinner. I just didn't know the important of education and it shows.

1982 at home thing ware back to normal, after school go into the house find a quick sneak and head to my new friends house to play football. They lived a couple building down from us. We would play till the sun went down.

## BASEBALL

1982 Home life, its summer time again, my brother 4 years older than I am, now has he has a life, so we don't hang out any more, now my best friend is my cousin, who livies in the project as while,

We are together every day playing on the swings just running around gym. One day one local baseball coaches sees us, walks over starts taking to us about gaining his baseball team. We said yes so we started playing.

1982 I really took a liken to game, my positions were pitcher, left fielder we practiced a few times and than season started, yes I was very nervous at the start, especially when I was in the out field,

1982 I was hoping the ball didn't get to hit me. When I was pitching, I was conferrable, just get the ball wind up and throw as hard as I could and throw pretty hard. Although I was wild meaning the ball didn't all ways go where it was suppose to.

1982 Hitting several batter, I found something very strange I a would always hit the girls with the baseball. which left feeling sorry for them. Theydon make any fuse over it they continued to play. Tough gars. That year as hitter I would walk a lot but strike out most of the time,

1982 I hit sixth in the line up that year. that year our team won the champion ship, after the season we had a banquet, where got trophies, and had lots good food. I will never for get that, I was hooked. I could not wait for the next season.

1982 I would continue to get batter, playing on the gym field with my cousin on the weekends and after school. So the next summer I was ready to play.

1982 this would be a very good summer for me, my cousin and I had a routing, we would go to the school, where they gave free lunches, play basketball from about 11am till 3 pm go home and play baseball with a couple other friends the rest of the day.

# CHAPTER 3

# "RAKE THE YARD"

1982 summertime, here where I think my father and I grew apart, we were sitting in the front room along with my mom and two other people, they talking as unusual, some body said that made me laugh, my father looked over at me and said "popeye get out of here listing to grown folks talk.

1982 Go rake the yard, with normal tone of voice, I got up moving slowly because I did not wont to rake the yard. I went and got the rake from the closet walked out side. and just stood there looking around. He could see me though the front door. So he repeated "rake the yard popeye. I got upset yelled some thing toward him throw the away and walked away.

1982 walked on the direction of my sister house because I knew he would come looking for me, so I detoured and went a different direction. I stayed out til 11pm that night, he was sleep when I got home. The next day when we crossed path the only thing he said 'I went over to your sister house looking for you"

1982 that was very bizarre. because I was expecting some kind of punishment. After that we never really talked until

1987. Although we lived in the same house. Go figure.

1982 I guess that meant no more fun trips to place like

## FUN PLACES

| Places | Taken by | Amount of times |
|---|---|---|
| 1. Amusement Parks | brother-in-law, friends | several times |
| 2. Race tracks | father | several times |
| 3. Fishing | brother-in-law | several times |
| 4. Zoo | schools | several times |
| 5. Pro Wrestling | brother-in-law | once |
| 6. Marineland | brother-in-law | once |
| 7. Movies | brother-in-law | once |
| 8. Parades | mother | several times |

## WATER HEAD

1982 The beat go's on "water head or Popeye bring me a cold glass of water", Yelling down the stairs at me, as he lay in the bed, after work, Or go to "store and get me a pack of cigarettes" At any time of the night. The cruel ridicule did not cease either, especially when I would be sitting watching television. Now, He was very disruptive.

## WATER HEAD.6

1982 junior high school time, I get got bussed to the san Fernando valley, which was a bit of a culture shock, I remember my first day attended class, the teacher chose me to be the ticket monitor, In charge handing out the tickets to students who answered questions correctly.

1982 At the end of class, I had enough tickets to cash in for prizes, how that can be when I did not answer any questions.

1982 I'm standing in front of the whole class, trying to cash in tickets. That everybody knew I should not had, the teacher said" give me those tickets, I know I can't trust you." The class laughed, I walked way feeling stupid. I should have know better.

1982 I thinking that's a good start at new school. If their kids around cover their eyes. For this part. As I understood it, if there was a class that you didn't like. You don't have to go there. You could hang out on the gym field or walk the halls till the bell rang.

1982 some bad advice that I took, I liked going there however; I just could not do the work in class room. Which left me feeling stupid? Every class I had was foreign to me. Once again turned any work of any kind. the class I would go to was home room and P.E.

## POVERTY, REALIZED

1983 I didn't know we were broke until junior school, when I noticed all the nice flashy things the other kids were wearing, shoes, clothes, coats, I most the kids paid for there lunch I had tickets. To me that was most embracing, I got used to it right away my stomach didn't care how I got the food.

1983 my wardrobe consisted of two or three pair of pants and two or three shirts. I average two or three pair shoes a year. some of those kids averaged that a week. As my dad would say "those kids have Charismas everyday." needless to say I became very disgruntled,

I wonted to quit school, But my dad would not let me. He made sure I got up everyday at 6am and He made sure got to the bus on time., He loved to humiliated me, going that valley school did just that. Every single day.

1983 I can understand why didn't make any friend. first thing I was not one the most articulate students and little bit withdrawn, which made it easy to misunderstand me. thus I struggled socially.

1983 I Thank God for sports, TV, music, a since of humor, support of los angels, ca and last but not least good health. Because I had nothing else going for me. At least that I could see. Those were the things that kept giving hope. 1983 Just a total misfit., I would attended there for one year a half. I would describe the experience as a good one, if I could have done the work it would been a great one.

1983 I got kicked out for an altercation with a kid, During P.E class in the door way entrance on the side of the football field gym. I don't really remember how it stared. And I don't had much of a memory of talking or playing with him. So I could not have had any type dislikes for him.

1983 The two think I remember, first, we were face to face, then we bumped together and a scuffle ensued. I applied a chock hold to him, which was a move my friends and I used all the time. And no one got hurt. And I had no attrition on hurt him. I never tried hurt anyone in my life.

1983. I don't remember how he fail to he ground, but do I remember stand over him as he as layer on grown. Spitting up saliva.

1983 I am thinking What did do, I am frighten wishing I could run away hide. The next thing I remember, Is one kids walking to me and saying "why did you do that"? I was speechless. That all can remember from that terrible day.

1983 I remember the next day being called for the home room to go the office, there I with councilor she advised me I was being kicked out of school. For that incident. she also told "that kids parents wont a lot more done to you ".

1983 I deeply regent not having to chance to apologize to him. Sincerely.

1983 I really enjoyed being on the campus, but I didn't care for the long bus ride. And getting up at 6am and getting home about 4:30pm, Coupled with the fact that was really lost in the class rooms and didn't any make friends. Made for a lost cause.

The diversity of the students was something I had never seen, making that the only good thing to come from the experience, Thanks.

# CHAPTER 4

## SCHOOL NUMBER 7

1983 Back closer to home lass of a culture shock. I fit in easily with the same attitude as before. I didn't take me long to friend, we both carried our folders in our back pocket, with one pencil, with no paper, so we hit off and were together all the time. We had three class together, In every class we would find a cozy spot in the back of the classroom.

1983 Let the games begin, we would play pencil break, however our favorite game was football. Yes football, first you have to clear the table, the object of the game, thump a folded peace of paper across the table, so it hangs off The table.

That's a touch down, than you get to kick an extra, by thumping the same triangular piece of paper though the goal post, the goal post was putting both hands together thumbs touching and the finger pointing up. as the other player tries to thump the football between them.

1983 In medal class the game was from an old cartoon show, blocking the doorways.

By stacking up, tables and chairs on top of each other. Sometimes my teacher would tolerate my behavior, other times he would send me up to office, however I would never go. instead I would go straight to the gym field. This went on for a whole year, of course I failed the class and all of the rest of them. I would attend there til high school.

## 1984 SUMMERTIME "YOU MUST BE CRAZY"

1984 MY MOM HAD TO BE THINKING? WHY IS HE NOT SHOWING INTERIEST IN GIRLS WHICH IS NATURAL FOR 14 YEAR OLDS. I LIKED GIRLS, HOWEVER; I WONTED IN CHANGE IN LIVE STYLE FIRST, YOU KNOW LIKE STABILITY. BESIDES WHAT DO HAVE TO OFFER. 1. IAM SCARED OF GIRLS, AND MIND WAS ONLY ON SPORTS AND FOOD, WHICH WE SEEM TO ALWAYS BE SHORT OF.

1984 SO WE WERE SITTING AROUND IN THE FRONT ROOM TALKING AND OUT THE BLUE SHE ASKS ME "Darron why don't you get a girl friend"

I answer without hesitation **"you must be crazy"**. That was end of the conversation.

1984 **summer time**, again same **routing** as last year, sports, sports. Free lunch, plenty on free time. Baseball season is here, we our same team as last year, so here we major

1984 opening day, League baseball style, the mayor of los angels was there to throw out first pitch, I will never forget got pleasure of shaking hand with him right he throw the first pitch. We played in the first game.

1984 The season started, and was I a much improved player, often hitting the baseball into preschool which in I straight away center field. It was ruled ground rule double because on the short distance. I developed a good swing and feel for the strike zone, so now a feared hitter. Also a much better pitcher with better control if my pitches.

1984 I was the biggest and one the oldest kid in the league, which gave me kind of advantage over rest the kids. They didn't complaint, we won title again. at the end of the season there was an all-star game, I didn't know it until my cousin and I was walking past the baseball diamond, the first thing that popped into my head, why was I not invited to playing the game? I know aim was one the better players in league, something I never figured out. There was a banquet and trophies ceremony like the year before,

## PRO BASKETBALL

1984 this year there was field trip after the banquet, to an NBA basketball game. Where got see a couple of my favorite players. It was one thing caused by me. I left my seat in the upper deck sneaking down to first deck. The true owners came to claim them. Little bit of a bummer But the experience was very memorable. Enjoyed it very much. Thanks

## "YOU BETTER KNOW WHAT YOU ARE DOING"

1984 Summer time as our relationship continued the deteriorate, here we go again, I'm sitting around the house laughing being joyful, I guess he was in bad mode which was normal. Now that he's out of work for good, He starts up with cruel ridicule. I start talking back to him with the same tone voice, something that I would not normally do.

1984 Normally I would sit there sad feeling sorry for myself. While caress me from a to z., but not today. So the conversation need up something like this, I wail get up and wipe you. before he just does it, without talking about it, I replied" you better know what you are doing". The conversation ended. **GO FIGURE.**

## 1984 HERE'S SOME OF THE FAMOUS CRUEL RIDICULOUS REMARKS.

"YOU AINT GOING TO BE SHIT"

"Son of a bitch"

"PUNK"

## THE COMPONENT SET, TV AND VCR.

1984 My mom purchased A television, Component set and VRC. for my room because loved music and TV, as while as movies, while that how I understood it. It also did one other thing replace sports. although I watched it every chance I got, I never thought about playing.

## BICYCLING

1984 My mother also brought a me bicycle which also help me forget about sports.

## LUCKY ME I STILL GOT SOME SANITY LAFT.

1984 I would spend about 85% of the next three years in my room. only going to school and bicycling. writing this reminds me of some thing I read in a book, yes I have read a book." It's no wonder he went crazy the wonder is why he didn't go crazy sooner". Lucky me I got some sanity laft.

# CHAPTER 5

## HIGH SCHOOL, NUMBER 9

1984/85 Ready or not here I come. It was not a big culture shock, when I first got there. I was little bit lost, I was use to being one of the baggiest kids in the school, here I'm just a regular 9th grader.

1984/85 I would find same problems, the inability to do the work, thus back to my regular classes home room, and P.E. Every time I decide to try going class would I get humiliated and discouraged.

1984/85 I still sported one worse wardrobes in the school. It seemed like I was the poorest in the whole school. And thought one of dumbest in school as while. During this time I really struggled with attendance.

1984/85 The great thing about high school, I guess they did have pities on me. because I got two books of lunch tickets every month. The one thing that really disappointed me was I did not qualify academically for the sports teams. One only real goal that had.

1984/85 One of the good moments, I will never for get, we went on a field trip to one the studios, to see one of my **favorite actresses**. From a very popular sitcom that ran 70s and 80s. Had great time, thanks.

1984/85 I would go there two years, however the 9th grade I would have to repeat, I could not believe it, I was being **held back**. I thought that crazy. That would not help my cause my education level was pre junior high school. The 5th grade was time I learned anything.

## 1987 ONE THE MOVIE AGAIN, NEW SCHOOL 9

We moved to different a part of town which I had not been to before, and school was not in walking distance so I had ride two busses to get there, same set up same routing. The thing about school,

1987 this the year I started driving, practicing in some my relatives cars, I caught on very quick. Drove well enough to where my dad allowed me to the use his car to drive to school. A old four door compact sadan. man, that needed body work.

However I drove it very proudly. It was like dream come true, dad letting me drive the car to school, I really could not believe it. I figured he was trying to be like the days, when we had good relationship.

1987 At this time he and my mom had broken up a few months prior to the start of school. while passing though the hall ways, I remember one of classmates walking up to me and said "man I seen driving a super bucket" slang for a beat up car. It didn't faze me, I loved to drive.

1987 I attend that school about two months, I seem to be wasting everybodys time. So I decide to quit, gym class wasn't enough to keep interested; plus catching the two busses. It just to much to go though for lunch and sports. 1987 Strike One, Starting life with without A High Diploma.

## 1987 OFFICIALLY A HIGH SCHOOL DROP OUT

1987 back to home and back tomy normal routin TV and music, however this time there one thing different. there people hang out in the front or our building drug dealers. So I started handing out with them. watching them sell, It I looked easy, it was fast money. So I started selling.

1987 First in front our building and than from in the house. I knew about the dangers of selling drugs after all it is against law. to this day I kick my self today for starting of that way, after I had seen what drugs do to people and no plans of ever getting involed in them. it was Definitely not for me.

I got arrested one month before my eighteenth birthday. I end up with six months probation. I did not know how much of a blessing that was to me.

## EIGHTEEN YEARS OLD

1988 My dad would help me get my driver license allowed me to use his truck for the driving test. I passed on second try. I WAS HAPPY

1988 my brother had a lady friend who lived a couple of blocks away, one day we walking from the store, He said Darron I wont you to meet my friend she lives on this block. I said ok, so we went over to large house, it was boarding house which rented rooms. we meet. started talking next thing I know one thing lead to another.

1988 She was **several years older** than I was, and on rock cocaine. She needed help so I let her move in, the first mistake.

Soon she was arrested and served about two months I went visit her several times and took collect calls from her. which ran my mothers phone biil up, something I could pay for at time. when she got out of jail she came back to stay with us. During this time she started talking about getting place together. tell me that things between us would be much better if we had our own place. So she tried persuaded me to start selling drugs again so we could move.

**In love,** I listened and start back selling drugs. From my moms house again this time I was lucky, I guess. I was not caught. So we moved out, Mistake number two. She and I both got jobs. she helped out on that front. And her self as while. I give her credit for that. She worked in the Medicare field.

1988 I worked as a security guard. Nether one of us could keep a job. She had cocaine problem. thus her problem was my problem, Making it mission impossible to keep a job. We were very unstable, all ways on the move. a total of four times, twice in los Angels twice San Bernardino, CA.

For some reason I could never figure her out, one minute she would be happy the next minute burning mad. Talking louding and acting violent while lead to many fights. Resulting in my being arrested three times.

We actually had some good times. Who ever for get the times we went to Westwood to the movies and shopping, Even though I was drove an old beat up four door sedan from 1973. the body was wracked, I remember driving thru Beverly hill and being advised by an office not drive thru there with it. She also advised me if she seen me again, she would impound it. As I was getting ready to pull off. She also gave me some more advice "you should just junk it". That was kind of funny. Any way back to Westwood can you imagine being an eighteen year old with kind of car?

Yes that was very embarrassing, but I had do what I had do. I remember buying my first car. I brought it at auction in the city of Paramount, CA. She was with me and helped pick it out, A 1979 big body four door sandan with sun roof top. chrome rims and big white wall tires. I had that car til was twenty five years old. Yes, I got lots of attention.

1988 this car was third one. in the one year, this was different I brought with my money which made it special. I test drove it. at the time I didn't know much about cars. thus I didn't know it had a bad transmission, luck for me my mom helped with some money along with my next pay check. I was able to get it fixed.

1988 Our relation was one sided, She made all decision she totally dominated everything. She knew because of my prior arrest. and having no where to go. I was at her mercy. So she took full advantage. All she would have to do is get loud, I would shut down. that was the routine when ever she wonted something to go her way… 1989 she would turn all of sudden. one minute sweet the next minute I hate you one day she started with normal bully routine. So I got up and headed for the door, at that point she picked up some type of object and begin striking my component set. the one my mother bought me five year ago. That started another fight which leads to yet another arrested.

1989 I remember going home one day. She seemed really up set she started talking about getting married. the reason was she gave "I don't wont to be living some body for years without being married. We had only been together for several months. I didn't wont to argue with her. So I said what thought would make shut up. Ok, I didn't know she had a plan for the same night, I thought it be feather down the line.

1989 She fooled me; she had a plan for the same night. I was shocked. I didn't to wont to fight, at the point that was going to be the option. I was trapped and railroaded into getting married. So we went over to an old means house. we were the only three there. There he preformed the ceremonies. And just like that I had gotten hutched. It took several years to get a divorce, when relationship ended I totally for got about it.

1989 After not paying rent and getting eviction on record, she moved and took me with her, after all you are not going to walk out on your new wife, I tell you, I felt like kid riding in back seat of a car the whole relationship. So we moved again this time to her mom's house in Redlines, Ca. once again we both got a job, so we only stayed there about three weeks.

1989 Than we moved to a room in San Bernardino, CA, than to apartment in down town San Bernardino. We lasted about one more month before another fight, this time started by her controlling violent attitude; so I got arrested again. and that was it, I had enough.

1989 Stike two and three; plus check mate all simultaneously, she had sabotaged every possible avenue out of poverty. for years to come.

1989 If I was a betting man, I would beat my house well can't say house because I don't have one and never have. I would bet you that she had a hidden agenda.

# CHAPTER 6

## BACK FROM SAN BERNARDINO

1990 So heart broken and every thing else. my wife wood not give me my second hand clothes, although I them purchased with own hard earned money. 1990 Upon arrival to back to the projects. The damages were as follow:

| | | |
|---|---|---|
| 1. Married for many years. | Separated | the stayed in the record |
| 2. Bad credit | one eviction | Filled bankruptcy |
| 3. Police record | Domestic violence | Ruin reputation. |
| 4. Bad work history | fired several jobs | unreliable. |

1990 So I naked fugitively of course I had my clothes that I had on. Lucky for me my allowed to come home because my brother was Hugh was homeless and she didn't let stay there 1990 So I'm back home with my mom with only my car. Depressed, and feeling just like a fool. That's obvious which any body could see. my mom ridiculed me and made jokes ha, ha. You got kidnapped and taken San Bernardino. she would say "I told you it would not work" which she did. So I knew not sit around and feel sorry for self. 1990 The next day, I went job searching. Lucky for me I found one in security. and started working the very next day. Something I found ironic, I went too picked up my uniforms. Maybe a half block, from where I got my first job, remember that nice young couple. On Lincoln street. Off Wilshire blvd 1990 For the next six to eight months, I guess I was still hang over from the break up with my wife, so I really did not wont start a new relationship. So I would go to work and back home everyday, on my off days, take my mom around to places she wonted go, mostly stores or visiting relatives.

## 1990 "THERE WERE A COUPLE OF MEMORABLE OUTING"
## FAMILY OUTING, TO THE BATTING CAGE

1990 somebody decide we should on a trip the local batting cage, both of parents, sister and brother-in-law, as while as my cousin, remember we played together in summers.

1990 I really struggled making contact, the bat seemed to be too heavy, and it was same size I use to hit with back in 82 and 83. However; my cousin was tearing the cover of baseball. I guess that ended any notion of baseball career.

## MAJOR LEAGUE BASEBALL GAME

1990 Another fun trip, It like the old days my brother law, it gave me flash backs. My cousin and myself, I bet could not guess where to. Yes, you where right, a major league baseball game.

## 1990 MEET MY SECOND REAL GIRL FRIEND

1990 I had girl cousin (RIP) who I grew up with. she and I was the same age. she lived in the project around the corner. she lived with her boy friend and little daughter. So In my spare time, I would go and visiting them on regular basics.

1990 that I began drinking and smoking. He and I became good friends, I also would take them place they had to go, since they did not own a car. One day he took me over to some of friend's house, where we listened to music and drank a few beers.

1990 DOWN STAIR LIVED TWO YOUNG LADIES THAT THEY NEW, THEY WHOULD INTRODUCE TO BOTH OF THEM, ONE OF THEM ME HITTING OF WITH, SO WE STARTED DATING REGULARLY, FOR A COUPLE MONTHS.

1990 SHE MET MY MOM ON FEW OCCASION, THEY SEEM TO GET ALONG VERY WELL. AND SO DID WE. THE ONLY BAD SHE DIDN'T HAVE JOB. AND WOULD KNOW IT, SHE ENED NEEDING A PLACE TO SYAY, NOW COMMON SENCE SHOULD HAVE TOLD ME THAT COULD NOT HELP IAM LIVING MY MOTHER.

1990 I WASN'T MAKING A GREAT DEAL OF MONEY. IAM LIVING WITH MY MOM SLEEPING THE SOFA. BEING THE NICE GUY THAT WAS. I ASKED MY MOM COULD SHE COME AND STAY WITH US. MY AS ALWAYS SAID "YES BUT ONLY FOR A SHORT TIME".

1990 WE WOULD STAY THERE FOR 6 MONTHS RENT FREE. TIL I COULD SAVE ENOUGH MONEY TO MOVE. IN THE MEAN TIME SHE WOULD STAY WITH MOM AROUND THE HOUSE. WHILE WORKED.

*1990 SO SAVED I ABOUT FIFTEEN HUNDRED DOLLARS. SO WE STARTED LOOKING FOR AN APARTMENT, BINGO, WE FOUND ONE IN HER OLD NIEBORHOOD NOT TO FAR FROM WHERE HER FRIEND LIVED WTH GIRL FRIEND. 1990 SO WE MOVED OUT, the deal was I pay the rent, WHILE SHE Pay THE UTILITS. WE GOT ALONG GOOD. FOR ABOUT YEAR two years, I GUESS BECAUSE I WAS WORKING LONG HOURS SIX DAYS A WEEK. AT A BANK. leave 8:30 return at 6:45 Saturday 8:30 return at 2:45. Sunday was the only day that we be together. during those hours.*

1991 there was a coincidence that didn't recognize, my girlfriend and my first wife both all of sadden need to move, both came to stay with me and my mom. they stayed at home with my mom while I worked to save for the move in money.

1991 my schedule left plenty of free time on her hands which she use to get back in touch with friends in the neighborhood, but she would be there when got off work. So it was never a problem.

1992 on my days off we would ride across town to visit my mom. and take her any place she had to go. Would have a few beers during the visit. And back home to ready for the next week. This routing went on for the better part of two years.

1993 we hit a bump in the road, the had ended so we re going to have problems paying the rent, I didn't have any money put away. so began to stress out. if we can't pay rent where can we go. It seemed be no options so, we decided to go or separate way.

1993 she moved back with her friend and moved with my mom. Mom had moved again but not far from where she uses to live. After about one month we were back talking. My mom really liked her. Mom definitely wonted me back with back her.

1993 we separated for about two months, then my mom got wish, again she allowed her to come back share the hideaway bad with me in the front room.

1993 back to work, this time in the valley at another bank, long hours again. This job would last about 6 month's. than it ended. That would be last time I worked with that company. I had no income and starting to smoke marijuana. with no way to support my habit. My mom would help me with first she would give money, she was disability so made her provider, that was little bit money compared to what was making on my job.

# CHAPTER 7

## I'M RETIRED

1993 a few month would go by, aim wondering if will ever work again aim 23 years old, I got be able to do something. Aim why can't I catch on to something Aim good at and liked to do that pays well. It seemed like I was an outcast or outlaw.

1993 Vie worked many jobs,. It like was not willing to work, I started thinking back to the jobs and places that I worked.

## TOUGH JOB

Asbestos worker, Century City, Ca. my least favorite job. I didn't like the conditions at all. You would have take off your all your clothes, put on a paper suit covering your entire body. Wear a oxygen mask fitting tightly around your head with the tank and battery taped tightly around your waist. Than go stand on scaffold scrapping away for hours. Was not my favorite job by any starch.

## IVE WORKED IN SOME NICE PLACES, SUPER MARKETS, BANKS, STUDIOS,

I've worked in some nice places, **super markets**, banks, studios, 1988 While at working in super market I got some of **best advise** ever given to from a store manager, I standing in parking lot, he walked out heading my direction, came up to me and said "I wont you out her working not shooting the shit with the customers and another thing don't date any body you work with, what if they come to work the next day and not happy? Turned and walked away. Yes, I did take that advice.

1991 to 1994 the **banks** was place was a really nice place work, after all you are guarding lots money and meting lots of people with money. Although I wasn't making a lot of money.

I loved the environment, mostly quiet, with many nice ladies, and on occasions and pot lucks. I was lucky to work with ladies from many different cultures. So I got the chance to meet them and try all types of foods.

1991 the **studios** was another place that I really enjoyed working. It had many perks. starting with all movies stars that you get to see, and work with And countless pretty women, thinking back if I would any gumption I would have got me one, two, or three. Of them. Although I worked long hours, the work is fairly simple just pay attention and know your duties. I did that for the most part. So why am I out of work?

I'm not like over barring or anything. I never asked for anything that I didn't deserve.

Like a vacation.

## COUNTY JAIL VACATION

I taken only one vacation my whole life. That only because I had traffic tickets that turned to warrants. Five thousand dollars Worth. I didn't wont to be pulled over on the way to work and taken to jail, and lose my car to the impound.

1992 I got three infraction by different agencies. So I would have to see three different judges. I was told it would be about three day's jail time. I don't have five thousand dollars. and my goal is to clear them at my convenience, I started talking the people I thought knew the court system. To see what the option were.

1992 I was advised that paying or jail time was the only way to clear them up. then Jail time it is. I went and turn my in to substation, which was design to cut one or two days of the jail time.

1992 every thing went to according plan, turned myself in, went court the next day seen the judge. Waited for the bus to pick up and take me county jail. The bus ride was little different than I was use to, the view wasn't very good.

1992 after a few stops, were here at place I've heard some many things about.

Ready or not it's show time. i put Into small hold cell packed with oyher inmates for hours waiting to go into next room. where everybody can see you naked, after that you are searched and given the county blue uniform.

1992 Now you officially in the in county jail. Next stop a very large dorm on top floor, 9500, where one the first things was I noticed was sign on the wall saying

# "PENTHOUSE LIVING AT ITS FINEST"

1992 I got into the penthouse, I stood in line to use the phone. I stood in the line for maybe thirty minutes. Once I got to the front of the line and reached for the phone here comes some guy out of no where to trying to grab the phone from my hand. I was not going let go after waiting the line. He let go of phone and walked away. after seen that we would fight over it. it was a test, I told that would happened. Although it still it upset me.

1992 I would in the be in the penthouse for about twelve hours than moved to a smaller dorm 9200. Much more quiet. At this point, every time is just like was told it would be.

1992 Surprise, I'm called for release. How can that be, I've only seen one judge. But I'm not going to mention it deputies, of course. Maybe the tickets have been dismissed. I didn't know what think. I know was just happy to going home. Needles to say, I didn't like they living arrangements any way. Not even the penthouse.

1992 I'm moved down stairs where there are several small holding cells, with hundreds of inmates waiting for release. I got moved from cell to cell, while waiting to hear my name called. I stayed there about 12 hours, finally, I hear my name called. so am moved to another side of the jail, which the last step before you are released, this part I was not told about.

9200 I'm was called for to release, I get the door and hold up. They found the other tickets, one of the deputy call me back. you got some more tickets. you got to go court tomorrow. Now I 'am burning mad. Because now I'm doing dead time. Meaning its a wasted day.

1992 I got back into the county blues. and than put into even smaller cell, shaped like a hallway. the kind you see the court houses. But much narrower. I'm still very upset. So I'm pacing back and forward. til this older guy says to me" sit down youngster before somebody steps on your toe and you get into a fight and get more time.

1992 That calmed me down. so we started talking. He said he had six months left and he getting out, as sat calmly. than he said look at him a young kid stand up holding his head down. He was only about eighteen year's old. about 5'4 no more than 150lb. he said "You are on short time".

(meaning only few days). (The kid) "He's fighting a murder case, which he(the kid) said he did, he's not getting out". I looked at that kid and felt very sorry him.

1992 on the way back though the system. I ran into a class mate for my last high school. He was fighting a murder case. I ended up spending spent a total of five day and half. and I still left there with a warrant, that they could not find it in the system. i went on my ownto clear the warrent. Something I should have done the first time. I learned two things pay your tickets, and the county jail is no place to take vacation.

# CHAPTER 8

1993 feeling more and more frustration everyday. I begin smoking marijuana everyday. Just to cope with having no life and feeling like loser. Needing money and piece of mind. At this point feeling totally stressed out.

1993 So one day my father was visiting with my mom the three of were talking outside in the front of the house, I don't remember if I walked or drove up. talking was something that we normally would not do. so I guess I need a fix because I was in very bad mode, I remember looking over at him and saying in loud cruel and taughting voice way **"I am retired."** and stood there looking directly in his eyes. a scene and words that wish I could take back.

## CAME DOWN SICK

1994 shortly after that he came down sick with cancer of the throat. I visited with him a couple of times at sister house while he was sick. my sister which I thank her for, asked me to do and say something that he and I never done to each other before I hug him and tell you love him,. I looked in his eyes I did see sorrow in them. I felt some worthy coming from him, he was in the last stage and had lost his voice. However; I did not feel much sympathy for him still.

1994 A couple months after he passed away. When I was told he had passed away by my girl friend I was sitting in my car playing music. I did not stop and did not faze me. Week leading up to funeral the I thought little him.

1994 When I went view the body at mortuary with cousin still had no emotion. The day of the funeral, I walked into mortuary and before I could get seated tears begin roll down my cheeks. I felt so hurt. I cried the whole funeral.

1994 at one time he was good father and a joy for me to be around. he spent lots of quality time with my brother and I. he took us out to many fun place. Like to park and beach and horse racing. I remember when we had dog we would walk the dog a to place called double dip a place with mountains, he called it rabbit hunting,

1994 although we never caught rabbit it was lots of fun just being with him. Also gave me my first bicycle something I still enjoy today. I remember in the seventy every Friday he would home a beg oranges something I looked forward to.

## PASSED AWAY

1994 the one thing he stood for honesty, respect. Discipline and taught it in a manner that knew how. It was the way he was raised. Most of the wiping was for my own good. I does think he was fair most of time. Up until early eighties. I would compare our relationship to profess wrestling script. **From partners to bitter enemas.**

1994 My father and mom seemed to get along just although they did not show a lot of love to one another at least in front of me. I only time I could them fighting was 1977or 78 while we lived Compton, more of a misunderstanding I guess, away the police were called they spoke to them both and left than thing went back to normal.

1994 However in the eighty things changed. he did not beat her but he was very abusive with words, he was out of work and struggling to support his habit of smoking and drinking thus; he seemed to be always be in mean sported. They did not show a great affection for one another during eighties. She didn't seem to take it to hard at all.

1994 to 98 I would continue to struggle keeping a job and housing. I would continue smoke and drink, but managed to survive. I would move from my mom house in 1995 only to return once one time, before she passed way 2004

## I SOLD MY CLASSICAL CAR.

That car has a special place in my heart. It represents so many phase of my life. It represented a young kid trying to be somebody. Trying the do right thing, It represented my first look at what life could be. I represented a person willing to work his up. It represented a kid with no education. Even though it painted negative a picture of me that was conspicuous and deceptive. The car had something that no other car I've owed had

### "SENTIMENTAL VALUE".

# CHAPTER 9
# "NOW I KNOW"

1998 while working as a security offcer, in paramount, ca a small city to the east of Compton, ca.

1998 I worked with an older guy by the name of Cheaster. He had a friend by the name of Don who wrote a bicycle. He would come around to talk with Cheater and myself. They had a friend who lived directly across the street from the security office, I can't remember his name all three of them approximately in there mid fourths.

1998 He had in head injury that was very recognizable, he spoke slowly but could you understand what he was saying, all he spoke about was his mother and their relationship. Saying how she hated his daughter and she had done bad thing to him.

1998 As I continued to work there I made friends with some of the tenants, one in particular she owed a flower shop, a few doors down from the security office, I would stop and talk with her when making my rounds. Her name was Sandy. She was very good friends with Cheater and Don.

1998 the three of them spoke frequently. I found Don and Cheater to be strange.

Starting with Cheater he didn't have any teeth and wore shoes with holes in the bottom. How did know? I noticed it when would sit down at the desk. He would kick up his feet on table, the holes were size of half of a dollar. He dressed kind like tramp and always wore the same clothes. And he didn't own car.

1998 Don wasn't any better, missing few teeth and dressed poorly and seemed to homeless, the thing that made they strange to me, they didn't seem to be on drugs or alcohol. They spoke very educational. So I couldn't figure them out.

1998 One day at work, During my patrol Cheater called me on the two way radio, tell me to come to security office. Speaking In authoritative voice. So I walked over to the office from across the street there were sides of the shopping center.

1998 I got to the office, walked in Chester was sitting behind the desk, don was also there, standing on the other side on the desk. walk in sat and down at the desk directly across from cheater, so we started talking I don't remember all the things we talked about any way the conversation turned in the direction of my body make up, my look. Face, and build.

1998 in a roundabout way that I was famous and everybody knew me. and face was very distinctive. He than summed up the conversation. By turning his head toward Don and said **"my mother hates my father"** which I think was directed at me.

1998 I got up and started walking back to my post, as walked past the flower shop sandy called me inside. I walked inside the door, than out the blue she asked me "who's on the hundred dollar bill".? Right than before answering. I know right that I was related to Benjamin Franklin. I went ahead and answered.

# THE EPITAPH

## The Epitaph of young BENJAMIN FRANKLIN

The body of B. Franklin, printer (Like the cover torn out and strip of lettering And gilding) Lies here, Food for worms. But the work shall not be lost; for it will (As believed) appear once more in a new and more elegant edition revised and corrected.

By the author.

I knew my back was strong but didn't think I could an elephant for so many years.

|  | **Bizzare** | |
|---|---|---|
|  | BORN | Dead |
| Benjamin Franklin | January 17, 1706 | April 17, 1790 |
|  | (170) | (170) |
|  |  | **DOB** |
| Darron Deshunn | Febuary 18,1970 | (One month) |
|  | (170) | (One day) |
|  |  | (Differents) |

I didn't only write my autobiography because I love to share my memories'. I wrote it to change the way some people conceive me. I won't be see in good way, I won't gain the trust and respect from the public. Hopefully this is a prelude to establishing an understanding with people. Thus opens doors and clears the way for **Success**.

## "THANKS"

Special thanks to the Los Angeles county library"Carson branch", in Carson, Cailfornia and it's outstanding staff members for making me feel at home.

Special thanks to Dell Computer for customizing my great computer and to Mircosoft Word for giving me the advanced tools.

**Thanks So Much**

# BOOK QUIZ

| Why? | What Was the goal | why was he told? |
|---|---|---|
| 1. I laugh too much? | 1. keep in poverty | 1. |
| 2. I was hard headed? | 2. Salvatage | 2. |
| 3. His up bring? | 3. Inprison | 3. |
| 4. The epitaph? | 4. payback | 4. |
| 5. All the above? | 5. All the above. | 5. All the above. |

Where do I go from here?

1.

2.

3.

4.

5. all of the above,

**There no wrong answer.**

Comments.

www.ingramcontent.com/pod-product-compliance
Lightning Source LLC
Chambersburg PA
CBHW070724240426
43673CB00003B/130